THE
APOCALYPSE AWARDS

T0360098

Nathan Curnow was born in Streaky Bay and now lives in Ballarat. His work is published widely in Australia and overseas, featuring in *Best Australian Poems 2008, 2010* and *2013* (Black Inc). His previous collections include *No Other Life But This, The Ghost Poetry Project, RADAR,* and *The Right Wrong Notes*. A winner of the 2010 Josephine Ulrick Poetry Prize, he is the father of four daughters and a regular swimmer of the pool's black line.

THE
APOCALYPSE AWARDS

NATHAN CURNOW

ARCADIA

Poems in this collection have appeared in *Australian Book Review, Meanjin, Best Australian Poems 2013, Overland, The Rialto* (UK), *The Australian, The Canberra Times, Rabbit, Mascara Literary Review,* the *Sun Herald, Cordite Poetry Review, Australian Poetry Journal* 4.1, *Poetry Monash, Another Lost Shark, The Wombat Vedas* (2011 Newcastle Poetry Prize anthology), and have been awarded the 2010 Josephine Ulrick Poetry Prize.

Others have been shortlisted in the 2013 and 2014 ABR Peter Porter Poetry Prize, the 2014 Josephine Ulrick Poetry Prize and Highly Commended in the 2014 Axel Clark Memorial Poetry Prize.

Thanks to the bright poets of my workshop group: Ross Donlon, Ross Gillett, Anne Gleeson and Lorraine McGuigan. Also to Melissa Howard, Anthony Lawrence, Paul Summers, Sean M Whelan, and my extraordinary family.

Cover Image and sculpture by Stephen Ives:
'Dolor (For Whom The Bell Tolls)' from *Bleak*, 2015.

Illustrations by Lily Mae Martin
'Insomnia' 2010 Ink on paper 60.00 x 65.00 cm
'Reduced' 2010 Ink on paper 60.00 x 65.00 cm

Australian Government   **Australia Council for the Arts**

This project has been assisted by the Australian Government through the Australia Council, its arts funding and advisory board.

First published 2016 by ARCADIA
the general books imprint of
Australian Scholarly Publishing Pty Ltd

7 Lt Lothian St North, North Melbourne 3051
tel: 03 9329 6963 / *fax:* 03 9329 5452
aspic@ozemail.com.au / www.scholarly.info

ISBN: 978-1-925333-56-5

to the gunshot thunder

'It is only our conception of time that makes us call the Last Judgement by that name; in fact, it is a court in permanent session.'

Franz Kafka, Zurau Aphorisms

'… and I sat in the dark, and thought: There's no big apocalypse. Just an endless procession of little ones.'

Neil Gaiman, Signal to Noise

THE LAST DAY
after Kevin Hart, for Phil Cousins

the last day will be etched on copperplate
free with sedatives in the weekend paper
picture a secular man at his letterbox—
in regards to your current emissions
Approaching the Great Migration (slogan)
there will be choirs and fog and strings
a dog named Nineveh will have finally escaped
a new mother will be searching for batteries
breathe but try breathing like something else
expect far less ash than you think
we know that many will want to face the sea
there will be a club gluing model planes
quietly like in the candlelight after curfew
just consider it a kind of eclipse
do not be late for the Stations of the Cross
there will be cooking without time to eat
lovers will return to the back seats of cars
you will write poems you do not understand
we urge you to bury some kind of treasure
to plant feathers to clasp stones and wish
the bang of a gate the ring of a phone
the cold bark of a dog in the street
the voices of trembling children singing
louder children louder like rehearsed

WELCOME

welcome to those
on their knees in driveways
posing crucified upon the concrete
to those of you rolling to the nature strip and back
in sleeping bags for sweat or comfort
though warned to be wary of sudden truths
it might be best to paint the house
they say Diet Coke is flame-resistant
wild spinach blocks the smoke beneath doors
in case there are snakes or if God be ears
leave some treats upon the steps
permit lovers to shag you harder than the novel
you're writing but can never seem to finish
swallow X but only if you swallow Y
individual results won't vary
there comes a new dialogue on breast cancer
unexpected and as always short-lived
and the broken hearted who make the most
of dying a little bit inside each day
will finally run through their own fingers
the blue that nothing comes out of

DEATH DUTY

we are all on it
getting promoted every day
constantly filling the vacancies
although nobody has much training
some start early on the preparations
while others don't see the point
every funeral service is a kind of debut
some are digging well into the night
tagging and turning for identification
the viewing of bodies is endless
we suspect that some befoul the dead
believers stroking holy cadavers
wreaths and crosses and casket sprays
there is always a wake to cater
prayers to be spoken at the ocean's edge
new blessings of smoke and fire
the hunt for the perfect farewell song
the rush on new range receptacles
accurate quotes on homicide clean up
the only industry in perfect health
everyone's tests come back positive
and everybody dies still at work
donating to a large scale public event
it takes a lifetime to escape

THE APOCALYPSE AWARDS

the night is especially irrelevant
but it's some kind of ritual at least
guests wear ribbons for 'living with futility'
aren't the stars all bound to turn out
talk of glamour and style and duplicate dresses
the red carpet is too bloody rich
small fires are being lit between the stalls
fist fights no one cares to stop
Should we celebrate? Yes! Now more than ever!
and that's when the host pulls out
the winner is Tango Defeats Depression
thanking God becomes a bigger joke
the orchestra is ready to drown on cue
train wrecks are so boring to watch
trophies are suddenly good for fucking
there's no end to the people who try it
somebody yells—*this could have been something*
then gives themselves a standing ovation
envelopes are laced with a lick of magic
people walk off in any direction
as if the memorial tribute is a good idea
when it's about to go on forever
there's no longer time for the usual breaks
the seat-filler union has disbanded
smoke and hissing and the big show stopper
go-go dancers in deadly heels
the only option being to turn it up
the after-party will go off without a hitch

XANADU
after the film directed by Robert Greenwald

for the attractive people
there is a wall to skate through
it was a joke until somebody told it
now every town mural is dripping red—
there is no talking sense to the ugly
some try the Biblical Diet to get into shape
or wear the breastplate of Saint Patrick
some couples get married before they roll
it's probably best if you're intoxicated
makes no difference if you like the movie
there are new spurts of red every day
you won't get through if you wear a helmet
it's a watermelon explosion if you fail
a place that so many of us dare to go
might be the mural on the toilet block
the love and the love and the echoes of
where neon tubes blink ultra violet
egged on by a fever that can't be denied
it's too late to unlock the secrets of fat
the runway is lit and bystanders waiting
what commentators say about your face

WINDSOR

no one resuscitates the Queen
she just slumps at the table so common
few have remained and everything spoiled
the arm she was trying to slip into her robe
ending with a puff of talc from the body
her attendant at the wall with the tray
but no gesture now not the slightest cue
the corgi-nose sausage going cold
a mast of light from the East Terrace
a final pageant of scattered pills
she was patron of the Calm Mother's Competition
until she threw lambs from the Tower herself
where are the trumpeters her amphibious ships
her subjects who lined the streets for hours
where is the Yeoman who stole her flag
and escaped down the Thames on milk cartons
finally—watch—the attendant comes
stepping through guillotined light
for the gentlest stroke of her unkempt hair
and a sip from the side of her cup
for the hand that ruled Britain—a souvenir
to be taken clean from the wrist
a steaming breath a sharpened knife
how it spills upon the cloth

DUEL

waking again with their hands around their throats
they haven't figured out what love is
she's wrapped in bed clothes and he's in a suit
unlocking the patio doors
kangaroos in the valley for the very first time
means nothing which means so much
a sodden joint in the ash tray on the photo album
the family snaps on the lake in the raft
she's rolling another as he loads the shots
the pistols and their timeless design
their end of life coordinator advises against it
preferring pills and a spritz with lemon
an epic finale to a thinning marriage
it's taken courage to lie this long
shredding the certificate was a real high point
the party balloons have been euthanased
time for the recording of their favourite actor
who they hired to count to ten
intoning the derelict upwelling of the world
the last text is too much for her thumb
pressed back to back like every night in bed
NFR in black texta across their brows
agreeing that the view was their saving grace
the hills and the breaking bound

AT TENDER TOUCH

mum locks the brothel and stops the clock
some unfasten their hooks and eyes
one picks up a glass then puts it down
and then tries to speak of fashion
cigarettes and orchids and beds upstairs
but nobody will return to those
there will be no more poses or introductions
still the rules about screaming and tears
the place could have done with a good dusting
she kisses the dolphin on her best maid's shoulder
there are pills and fans and half smiles
pocket mirrors no one can bear to clip closed
though one keeps fiddling to release herself
her girlfriend staring through the rusted bars
remembering the time she vomited blood
in a wedding dress worth ten polishes
mum graciously takes the clock from the wall
for once nobody wants to face it
we swallow her gifts without a gag
and curtsey like the bomb

CORPSE FÊTE

the corpse selling kisses at the kissing booth
a corn pipe jammed in its mouth
packed with mundungus and blue cheese
to overpower the stench of flesh
every stall holder is on ropes and pulleys
figurines in some dark fundraiser
two women at the urn in the coffee tent
in mittens to hide the blisters
a fumbling of tongs at the sausage sizzle
balloons tied to the clown's remains
every lucky dip is a gift wrapped finger
the face painter is receiving complaints
the stiff on the gate of the animal nursery
the dead float in the dunking chamber
red velvet cakes cannot be trusted
or the draw of the meat tray raffle
the fortune teller has dropped the ball
the sponge throw takes out an eye
nobody cares that they can see the ropes
no one finishes a whole toffee apple

NOSEBLEEDS

every tissue soiled and scrunched
to the size of a tight carnation
the paint inside us making a break
some juggling the drops on bank notes
spilling on the keys of the saxophone
upon the trays at the fast food chain
on every feeding breast and baby's face
the deli meat colour in question
others find a way to ignore the drip
erasing all shades from their palette
as docile as guide dogs at traffic lights
they watch grey turn grey then walk
others have dubbed it the 'cherry run'
a last communion for all to share
while cardinals eat crab in crimson bibs
noses pinched as they spread the butter
they tell us somebody stole the idiot fruit
they say make it all up for yourselves
did we all get a whiff of Murdering Point
who suggested we lick the toads
as it pours into the cup of every hand
the pilot leaking before the crash
no lights to guide us to exit doors
the inflatable slide the rush

SÉANCES

teenagers help their parents conduct them
in exchange for car keys and weed
but if they tire of quizzing the Ouija board
the pointer just keeps on moving
packed away the wooden heart slides faster
knocking against the sides of the box
some wrap it in blankets and stash it in a draw
some submerge it in a tropical fish tank
an anonymous narrator dictates *War and Peace*
and the back story of the Cheshire Cat
something is spelling *quality mince matters*
perhaps a butcher with undying remorse
this last parlour game this after-life rhythm
a constant tapping of fees and charges
Rosabelle-answer-tell-pray—believe believe believe
over and over from beneath the house
wedged in a locker at the Ever Fit gym
abandoned in a food court at an empty mall
the dead metronome counting down
some set it on fire to watch their flaming souls
posting premature messages from the grave
others never tire remaining stuck to the board
for answers that will come soon enough
as the family car pulls out throbbing with bass
denouncing the beats of the Angel of Death
the last players of hip hop middle fingering
the stereo uh yeah uh uh uh

ESCAPOLOGY

the last global craze
locked bags and hairpins
misguided cracks at contortion
buildings set alight for escape attempts
there's barely enough time to practise
so many aspiring 'modern day Houdinis'
house pets being trained as assistants
steel boxes are dropped into icy rivers
a necropolis of boxes still shackled
the illusion we can escape from anything
strait jackets and burning ropes
some of us work as Torah magicians
others pray to Saint Nicholas Owen
tanks and barrels and waterfalls
a mad rush on police issue handcuffs
the danger is real but the chains are not
an excuse just to end it all topless
the 'milk can trick' with live piranha
someone tied in blue tentacles knots
as if only the masters will have a chance
when the great vaudeville comes to close

SUBMARINE

he's converting the house into a submarine
there are so many corners to curve
watertight living is about the rivets
and the library needs more Jules Verne
the tv remote works the climb and dive
the mute button engages stealth mode
ceiling fans are his propulsion device
he can be seen through a portal window
rewarding himself with fish and chip Fridays
loading torpedo tubes with junk
falling asleep in front of deep sea docos
buffing his downpipe periscope
was he a cabin boy in another life
does he need a reason to wear pirate shirts
perhaps all of this is about some girl
now he's testing his breath for fog
there's the thermocline to think about
and his octopus has outgrown its tank
but imagine steering the Mariana Trench
listening to The Best of Kenny Rogers
to a cave somewhere that's a perfect fit
where it can't hurt to power down
all that colour in the dark beyond
the reasons never spoken

THEATRE

a gnashing of teeth that seems to work
although the intention is hard to swallow
every musical number is a vomit of swords
the red curtain tears itself up the middle
the fourth wall collapses on the audience
a great hurling of things from the apron
even now it's hard to tell if there's an interval
somehow the sweet smell of shit wafts in
better casting can be seen at the local tip
and the lighting rig accident is bogus
there's no doubt surgery is a kind of theatre
but the trepanning operation takes hours
the monologues are heavy and lead off track
script-wise it should not have got up
the costumes are to die for in *every* sense
wash to wash it just doesn't look good
a daring tribute to unfunded excellence—
says the director's mum in the program notes
a boxcutter murder helps create an edge
see the gnashing is the bit that works
the gyrocopter crash is predictable
set design from dynamiting a clam
no spoiler alerts as it can't be restaged
three stars—I prefer adaptations

CHRISTIANS

Christians go from coffee to praise
then break into small groups to share
Kingdom Rule—What It Means For Your Super
drive thru baptism at the window
a blessed moist towel and free beverage
pets must travel in ark shaped containers
you can all read about it the Olivet Discourse
of course the discourse is best discussed
in trains of logic and acceptable thought
there is last minute training on both
born again to talk in a manner of speaking
pocket bibles with meticulous footnotes
new translations in a range of covers
rubber thimbles help turn the pages
praying for those about to get messy
in the coming reign of the messianic
the Scripture is clear on ungodly acts
how Sodom took Gomorrah from behind
and cities will be smote with holy fire
if all they drink is decaffeinated
this is the way to give God the glory
what Jesus really meant when he said
try another sweet biscuit of the bible belt
raise your hands up and come down the front

THE GURU

his rants make sense with 'listening glue'
he's convinced he can poop a dove
prophesying how a dragon will shake the building
separating the wheat from the chaff
murderers go to hell and play Cluedo forever
salvation—harder than pissing on a frog
we dig him a moat and fill it with lions
'hurple' is the mantra of the month
he blesses each raid on the cannery outlet
gives us hair bracelets and Kalashnikovs
flexible parentage is the number one doctrine
everything is consensual at first
exactly how much sun will bleach a camel
tepanyaki is your mum—
his koans are unique and so expensive
they are impossible to forget
passing the time with games of wink murder
while he sleeps in his celestial vault
it's his destiny to ascend in a skybox we bought
with the life savings of non-believers
rejoicing when the famous clown becomes a convert
until we grow wary of tricks up the sleeve
we patrol the stockpile and then the orchard
executing the voluntary penance
and when the guru returns trembling on stage
trying hard to poop one with wings
we see it all makes sense in his divine program
on guard for whoever smirks first

THE ANGEL

we queue up to kick it between the legs
a new test we've devised for the herald
though its eyes shine bright as temple fire
though its tongue is a righteous sword
some are expecting the clang of a cymbal
or the sound of a Nepalese bus crash
single mums are choosing to group together
for a 'Women's Only Spectacular'
as it grips the pole beneath the basketball ring
as people step from the free throw line
Boy Scouts hope for a last-minute badge
Furries are dressed in full fursonas
does its face screw into a bad cartoon
like some poorly restored fresco
will its message fall out and onto the court
spilling like lollies at a child's party
here come the Cancan girls to the target
this is how they step to the chorus
each punt the tone of a water logged football
not a ripple of a shiver through its feathers
each striker returning to the back of the line
although the deal is one person one kick
enter the crow with a jet black flash
and the crow says *hark hark hark*

TIDY TOWN

paddocks of hay bales as neat as jam rolls
or stacked like lamington fingers
here is the spire and here is the steeple
the committee waits and winces
butterflies trained to thread the air with welcome
the cemetery cleaner than a private school
green courts forecast a new age for tennis
every barbeque light is operational
there is a standing arc of debutantes
and the cops' three piece big band
a bugle misfires at the one minute warning
flushing out the syphilis rabbit
an argument about whether to oil the windmill
or to let it complement the silence
the sham bible study in the sham rotunda
thrashing out the book of Revelation
the owl says *who* the pussycat says *me*
the breasts of the mayor's wife collapse
everyone's struck by mobile phone blindness
and the irrelevance of loyalty points
it's too late to redirect the judging panel
now it's nothing but an organised slum tour
past the decorated tree that killed the teen
four horsemen in the avenue of honour

BACK PADDOCK

a bag of mixed lollies at the edge of the desert
three inbred siblings with beaks
a fight for milk bottles in the wreck of a car
everything comes down to elbows
Jethro picking non-stop at the crust of the dash
what was once such a biblical ride
I'll fuckin whack ya Jethro like dad did that time
in the lymph glands remember that
as the radio crackles like the exploding gum
that bursts in their open mouths
a meteor descending with a Betadine glow
amid broadcasts of the Death Book
like a morbid throwback to the Drive-In days
as recounted by their blustering dad
the hundreds of women he supposedly laid
imprinting them with leather grain vinyl
a red Starburst in a clammy hand
Jethro climbs to the top of the bike jump
out there where he launched the roadkill's guts
his brother and sister can get fucked
pissing down the ramp just to watch the stream
choosing a new rock to throw back at them
fooling around with each other when he's not there
fumbling all the family shit

TROJAN HORSE

we build it with pallets and biscuit trays
and the satellites that fall to earth
it doesn't seem right without people inside
everybody puts their name in the draw
we consider it a kind of celebrity marquee
gaining entry is the only point
it stands in the rot of the raw sewerage
seeping out between its boards
waiting for someone to roll it away
we christen it Jejune Jejune
sometimes we can hear its belly groan
crying out like a distressed piano
we prepare a lecture on human ponies
to be followed by an offering of apples
breath steams out when it's freezing cold
and its eyes are always upon us
might even be worth trying to start a war
or performing the sacred sex magic
instead we push it to the top of the hill
in the light of a false white rainbow
now it's waiting beside the apple tree
this dumb horse prop without a rider
a new charge building upon the plains
somebody has to take it

METEORITE

it turns the face of the barn fed owl
calls the chill of grandpa's ghost
the cabbages glow as the bulb comes down
it plays the reeds of the smokeless marsh
shining like satin flung out from the roll
and the world is khaki and shadow
and the world lies pickled beneath its milk
the holler and the hoot and the cradle
he catches its voltage skipping the river
finds it boiling beyond the blackberries
it knows no future and no secret stars
plays no hint of an alien broadcast
collecting it with a pair of salad tongs
showing it the first of his magic tricks
he sniffs it for clues of its galactic journey
then wraps it in a tea stained cloth
he knows that the hunt is coming his way
and that mama has intestinal worms
he hides it in the belly of a gutted frog
that fizzes from the mouth then explodes
together they elope to the chicken coop
he reads it Gilgamesh and Ozymandias
mama is drunk and the bugle sounds
it is the great sleeping god of the age

ZOO

keepers lure the apes with banana trails
and euthanase them in a cold room with cake
the others are freed to the merciless wild
of raiding vandals and child soldiers
the alligator waits beneath the carousel
baboons dream of ripping off faces
the anaconda is the shape of a baby seal
and dingoes are walking bike racks
the elephant's trunk is full of fire crackers
the fairy penguins are on lollipop sticks
spoonbills are being used as cutlery
in a tea party with lemurs as servants
every encounter is a 'phobia session'
the giraffe was the first beheading
they tried using its neck as a periscope
the meerkats saw it all and worried
swans modified into wind instruments
wombats rolling like oil barrels
the jaguar wakes after sinking so low
on the table in the animal hospital
the eco-inflected panda nursery burns
the elephant's trunk is about to explode
baboons are wearing the faces as masks
the baby seal is reducing slowly
the jaguar groggy from anaesthetic
passing out between the roots of a fig
a detonation rolling across the park
the camouflage of fallen leaves

LEGOLAND

they recreated Anne Frank's hiding place
actual size built block by block
it's somewhere between the Lego Sphinx
and the London Bridge collapse
a secret door with enough clutch power
since the Mindstorm program went rogue
the Lego Robots are patrolling the park
overpowering the foreign tourists
chaos erupting at assembly points
the fracture of kingdoms and wonders
icons toppling and mini figures
babies sucking on spaceman helmets
a tsunami of bricks and disconnect
every step is a barefoot nightmare
and kids who enlist in the Robot Youth
don't have to clean up their share
the surveillance of sensors and actuators
a laser scanning beneath the crack
a rot of stowaways hushed and hungry
the non-toxic six-stud blocks

LIBRARY

we barricade ourselves inside
and select the best reader among us
what's the point of protecting all these books
if they're not being read by someone
we have shelves and banners and bean bags
desks stuck with all the gum we can stomach
we're a dedicated chapter of bookish guards
trading cigarettes for sets of bookmarks
10 Ways Reading Will Save Your Life
although everyone knows what's coming
a mix of *The Road* and *World War Z*
plus *A Hitchhiker's Guide to the Galaxy*
we're taking our stand among the titles
because we feel powerless without them
our natural tendency is to romanticise
imagine the fire at Alexandria
we have popular weapons for medieval war
and a whiteboard for emergency use
a catalogue search and we're off to find
How to Take Hostages for Dummies
our reader consuming an array of genres
stacked in a makeshift literature fort
the sentence coming is overdue
we don't like endings full stop

BOTANICALS

one bulb strapped to the back of each head
every family wants to go their own way
the bowls of our skulls will make perfect pots—
the window of survivability is broken
put your trust in deep sleep therapy
expect the colour of a licorice plague
here comes another of those Learish storms
welcome the negatively buoyant swan
there is no us & them there is only &
parents *should* have to bury their children
no one expected jousting to make a return
or the Tyrannysauras of distance
the intickable untockable annihilation
the helicopter culling has begun
dogs are sniffing cancer and spiked tofu
zombies escaping the Allergy Institute
hear now the primitive streak of our Lord
all people want to do is save Christmas
our dollars will soon stay local forever
and everyone's bios are forthcoming
the divinely violent weather event
all the shadows of a manta ray hot spot
think general rule of thumb and tall soft stems
the pointed end of the bulb should be up

POPULATION

another bleach attack in a failed state
no General wants to talk in specifics
men in blue helmets ride white Toyotas
nonsense and war are lovers
gaming tycoons in tuxedo t-shirts
everybody drinks paint like champagne
no beast of the water or dark matter
the Apocalypse is all population
Gen Y jihad flamethrowers for kids
battling the five diseases of hunger
wartime presidents are hiding in yurts
germ protocols have been abandoned
someone broke into the seed bank again
a new weapon of metastasised wasps
a peppering wind of fire and sulphur
the unorthodox deformations
shamefaced deniers and doomsday rape
suicidal ideology for the masses
the final genre—mediocre bang bang
kids are the reason for bullets

DAWN

it's just so big we don't get it
the slow milk of it the fat swamp of it
the subscription with pictures and everything
the curtain swollen at the open window
the pale wafer upon the tongue
that distant smoke or Lazarus unwinding
award-winning cinema in the making
a landmine beneath a pride of lions
a rowboat from a marvelous city
that hauled itself across the telephone wires
upon the birds upon the telephone wires
the good yolk broken over knitted hair
the mirror that's forever burning
a megaton-bomber or a bridal-train
the open mouth of a child running
and Jesus loved the little children
but there were just so many of them
until in light of what we sang to death
it became our greatest forgetting

THE LULLABY PREGNANCIES

1. TWO BLUE LINES

Team Love will arrive with pregnancy tests
requiring compulsory participation
introducing the term 'lullaby pregnancies'—
this implausible wave of conceptions
it came before locusts and deep image colour
world's end—a cinematographer's dream
when all I ever did was touch myself
to recorded whale music
PREGNOW-PREGWOW in a large envelope
10x Urine Collection Cups
a pregnancy pack with 25 strips—
it's all about caring isn't it
crow the stones and savants
actors roam the streets in character and flak jackets
while choppers chime above the city
looters are scoffing chocolate biscuits
wait for an outbreak before visiting the toilet
mask the tearing of the plastic wrap
they return for results with perfect motivation
and cigarettes to see if you'll smoke
they stare you down like Scientologists
before they laugh and say—*laugh to live longer*
to test your virginity they will sing Hosannah
and the Jesus is Coming Again medley
I've kept the impossible two blue lines
but destroy it if you can and the cups
everything you do will be considered suspicious
laugh and light up then laugh

2. BLOSSOM

no one blames a tree in its final season
for blossom that outdoes itself
the world remembering what it once did best
before giving up all together
it's time to clean the house again
how full the term to come
my washing basket no longer hugs my hip
I hold my hand with my other hand
every day a coat-hanger appears at my door—
an invitation a threat a promise
I've taken the photo of mother from the wall
because even she was watching
the Mercy Rule has been revoked
I've denounced Wicca in all its forms
butterfly twangs are the cells embedding
or thunder through my furniture
their disaster plan is a fitting disaster
it's a tribute to throwawayism
people piss on cave art and in shop windows
on anything resembling the Nativity
everyone busy with high pollen updates
sharing thoughts on overdose
message undelivered in 5 days 0 hours
any assembly is branded as 'coven'
there is blood to blood contact
and backpacks full of nails and ball bearings
to scramble the wire between my legs
even the coat hangers are breeding

3. TEAM LOVE

we're blaming the midwives hunting them
they're stripped and dunked to one hundred
we set traps—a woman full-term on a platform
every new-born baby another riot
they armed themselves so we spread more lies
we hang placentas in trees for the morning
as if mothers have to save them from being eaten—
the price of these glorified doulas
still they move among us attending somehow
with carving knives—they always cut
they bend women over and jam anything sharp
into the spine—call it an epidural
mothers accusing mothers swearing inducing
their breath stinks of methylated spirits
every child they deliver must be named 'Antigone'
they fill women with stones then suture
still they move among us attending somehow
those we catch have questions at first
they look so tired and straight at us
as if we know why so many are pregnant
we score their limbs and they confess it all
until we believe their stories ourselves
and because we believe we score their limbs
they welcome the ecclesiastical penalty
we're blaming the midwives hunting them
now their role is overrun
every tree adorned every new-born baby
the flesh we hang above us

4. STORKS

life-like violence graphic
the shots sound closer to home
they're shooting the storks until it makes sense
claiming stress-relief combat fun
but the babies keep coming
and nobody knows why on earth it ends like this
with a plague of births in our final orbit
proof that shit magic happens
families tie knots in their own pyjamas
there are workshops for the self-help kind—
How to finally accept your own private grunge
Buddhism for mothers with school children
but they're shooting the storks burning their nests
anything with a twinkle in its eye
speaking of disguises I've nothing to wear
except free-flowing baggy clothes
everyone turning like a gypsy thief
the streets are a plank to walk
people drink bin juice for some kind of resistance
and tails make whirling dervishes of dogs
nothing but everything in high rotation
the world is a dangerous discount sale
push the word I'll whisper to myself
no more posts to match my query
no more digging for survivors
just shooting as if it's the last curriculum
boys on concrete pipes outside my window
are playing at staring like spies

5. BUNKER

for you myself I clawed the dirt
sometimes I licked my fingers
I've a sharp boiled knife the cleanest towel
the gas lamp I'll hiss along with
calm now I must be calm like hypnosis
my ticking foot my swelling feet
as if from this end I can make a life
my shimmerfinny poppet calling
a deck for Solitaire and a daisy pressed
to hold beneath your chin when you arrive
though there'll be no light for forty million years
I'll still say—you like butter
when to close the hatch and deliver us
every Matroyshka doll has been destroyed
duckless lakes are full of broken bread
and every skull wears a frown
no one can afford 'unforgettable'
the world gripping waiting like shit
pear shaped now for growing pear shaped together
beneath a fire that never cures itself
pulsing already with the hint of burial
the bunker stocked with every good
a helium balloon as a treasure of laughs
on your birthday if we can inhale it
the countdown clock is flashing HELP
be my girl with a heart shaped face
the daisy pressed a sharp boiled knife
the gas that sounds like this

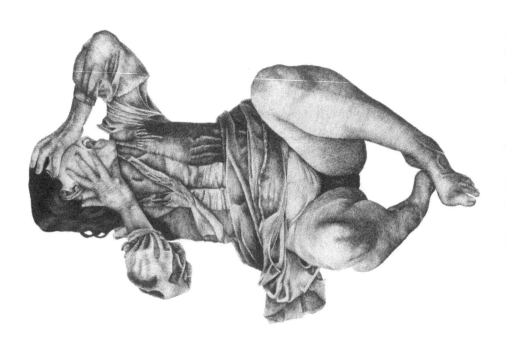

RED SHAWL FLAPPING

there are not enough flowers and the wolves close in
a baby wakes in an empty house
a splash upon the doorstep and a red shawl flapping
but nobody heard the shot
strands upon the spade that remains unhidden
a plot of earth beneath the pines
the moon comes chanting at the broken gate
the rope puzzles remain unsolved
cicadas sizzling above a war of wheat
sparrows revel in the dirt-bath dust
a television turning the milk upon the bench
toward a slow bold hunter's nose
and the baby the chanting a red shawl flapping
on the grim slack whip of the line
a racket of carriages passing in the distance
everything gets dragged outside

SHADOW GANG

a pouncing fox and wicker basket
at the deckle-edged lip of the lake
the pie is gone and the cream has spilt
the heels of the loaf have hardened
deep are the tracks that leave the path
broken is the branch and arrow
quiet is the mouth of the stony well
and the witch inside the chapel
her black pouch full of wild dog rose
a soap giftwrapped in ribbon
the broken bones that won't reset
the hasty backyard branding
torch fire fuelled by the holy lard
the bridge and the protestations
a stamping freeze and belt of cloud
the groan of the rope left hanging
a silent watch from the other side
a shadow gang on a high cliff wall
the standing oars that say 'keep out'
the softly softly snow

WHIMPERING STUMP

a wooden doll that danced the board
the swing bridge across the chasm
sharp is the lip of the leaning axe
red is the waste in the bucket
wheeling the wick of the kerosene lamp
the deer head mounted on junk
dark and deep is the offal pit
a whimper at the whimpering stump
somebody botched the circumcision
the boy locked inside the shack
a fang and claw is a briefing note
the keyhole packed with chestnut
playing the tune as the rocks reheat
thyme oil to coat the blade
a galloping pulse behind the door
the three day mess and mend

GIBBET

a herring bone is not a key
killing time takes real devotion
the iron clutch of the cadaver cage
the threat of swooping season
piratical frost and lost comeliness
a plea and a swing and a rattle
every prayer is a rock to the head
every pilgrim is a highway troll
lightning strikes the diamond mine
turning the lavender field to toast
the burning itch of hairy blossom
pressure sores and a collar rash
a hawker leaves his business card
a sedan chair's parting curtain
a walking wizard who is not a wizard
at anything else but walking
three black birds on a single branch
a snake trapped in the mouth of a can
writhing only makes it worse
the bars of its belly skin

HAWKER

a hawker selling nylons no one wants
reciting lines with a puppet voice
sale or no sale there must be a show
it's always a good time to plant garlic
the organ trade has bottomed out
the lewd woodcuts are going cheap
this thing might be a shrine to seafood
this towel sponges everything up
today dodging arrows is an elite sport
tomorrow will be a tower of tumblers
the poles have tipped and tip again
there are more hate figures than effigies
cicada sex toys are so yesterday
people moaning to get what they want
everyone says they are part of the show
moral—never play knuckles with a monk

SIKH

a sikh is hiding in the sugarcane
the threads of a stress soaked shirt
a ripening cage doesn't make a jail
the carpet python has woken up
a lopsided hiss from a cleft palate
the fresh leak in the storm water tank
tossing beer bottles at the humpy cow
a new heron bridesmaiding its back
the field is sighing like a wanted man
the bishop has been compromised
a star chart full of twists and turns
the wedding will not be cancelled
a slow truck enters with big explosives
someone is collecting the chains
betting on who can find him first
next is the cow and the feast

GARDEN MAZE

a morning mouth of pebble mix
lost somewhere beneath the bench
a hangover inside a garden maze
the fountain and a roaring piss
who shot the arrow that's stuck in his arm
the sheriff or the sharpshooter clown
the apple beside him is a kind of clue
every apple is an apple museum
every dead end a cigarette—no lighter
the sun dial says time is short
he barely recalls stealing a sprig of mint
the bum note of his band in disguise
a voluptuous nude with tipping jar
and a new white rabbit to follow
flames licking over the high hedge walls
what those with the fire know

TALLY STICK

a pocket clock in ticking ash
the red dragon cinnabar beads
rifling the ruins of the tally stick fire
the alphabet slurry in the sluice
burning scripture is everywhere
a melted face stuck to the bridle
pans of balance and marmalade pots
the sound of a distant motor
the rocking track of a rocking horse
a typewriter with melted keys
a bald paintbrush and rolling pin
the cat still chained to the grave
charred to a pungent charcoal roast
jaws stuck in a ceaseless hiss
the motor is dribbling closer now
someone slicing their thigh for relief

CAVE (FROGMOLL)

the frogmoll tries to hold his tongue
before the engravings of a hate-filled race
the poacher has finally lost his way
groaning like a horse down a mineshaft
the pool overstating its mysterious light
with a fresh interpretation of bones
a drip peeling down the frogmoll's back
the banana freckles don't rub off
the long echoes of a lumpen world
bulging with murk and promise
the mineral walls could use a lick
and the vaginal rock formation
the next poacher is just a tongue away
it's written in symbol and verse
drip and the bud of the drip to come
nothing from the frogmoll's mouth

MINOTAUR

the snort and rummage and fictitious drool
the horns and the wheeze of a shadow
a huddled bulk of gloom at the end of the bed
a snuffed candle with a turning tail
genitals in the mirror appear closer than they are
the burrowed eye and the endless hall
there is no left or right only forward and down
the omen of a triple moon halo
here comes a reference to the ball of thread
here stalks the evil that ponders man
the warning kazoo was blown too late
and the motion sensor frog is rubbish
a cold reading of a diary at the end of the dorm
stroking the curls of his rufflewool chest
the monster amazed is a maze reference
what the bully with the cattle prod did
the turning tail and smashing fingers
as he returns to the keyboard again
the mirror disclosing this is not a drill
weeping at his own reflection

LIGNOCAINE

a lock jawed sailor in a dentist chair
with a riddle and a mermaid squirm
the open casket upon the dock
the silk shirt that caught the bullet
here comes a rolling sponsor of clouds
hear the *plink* of the stainless hook
the face tattoo is a treasure map
every teardrop marks the spot
where rivers run and oceans fall
and the world is a teetering tray
the burning harp inside the storm
where the conqueror holds the baby
as the pink river dolphin lifts the rock
as the cumulus climbs with the gull
the dentist testing the nerve of the gum
the flame that paints the needle

SCRIMSHAW

mustard wind at the end of the beach
a woman with a scrimshaw face
she lifts her skirt and the sea foams in
with a colourful flotsam of plastics
a mouthful of ping pong turtle eggs
harvesting swells and mashers
turbines exploding above the dunes
a blotch of squid ink mayonnaise
trapped in nets of virgin hemp
a blowhole scoops a breath
a camel is spitting an oakum gob
re-stitching the sea mist seam
the skip and the tingle tug of a line
the salt rash between her legs
cookie cutter sharks biting o o o
the sea shanty sings itself

PREPOSTORO

the celebrants name is Prepostoro
a wedding under cliffs of shale
an audience of washed up skeletons
polished clean of the oil rig fire
the groom is gnawing on driftwood logs
the bride with a mid-west blow wave
her bouquet of thistles flowering fish
the boson and the dead letter love note
rings and a kiss of wind lashed lips
the signing of a crust stuffed pheasant
a hasty defecation in a pricklemore squat
beside a washed up blow up mattress
the stinging confetti of a crumbling cliff
a consummation between beached whales
the dark lup lupping of royal waves
the golden fog of fairytale

THE LIGHTHOUSE

nuns are eating plastic bags
their cathedral has rolled down the hill
it's a dinner party with a touch of cancer
what the tongue magnifies in the mouth
they tried storming the lighthouse again last night
they plan to fill it with animal pairs
the world is burning like a hoarder house fire
and the lighthouse keeper enlisted
exactly how did he survive the balcony fall
are we talking about the war or the riot
nobody trusts the town alarm
nuns are running in religious habit
past Junior who keeps his arms outstretched
so when he dies he can meet the Red Baron
Fran bottles her delicates to throw in the sea
if she can stand after all the red wine
we can put it all down to nocturnal asthma
because the nuns have gone fucking nuts
Junior says the lighthouse keeper can fly
he says *it's simple he just goes like this*

THE KEEPER

he turns from third to second to first person
I see the town in the butt of the mountain
an orchestrated rally without bells or drums
the stars that she drew into monsters
she left me for the barracks of fresher battles
when my head was full of apricot storms
ten thousand ships now she is all I see
in a dream sequence of galactic events
I will ask her to take me for a military man
remind her of my moon spotting eyes
although everything appears to see me first
the beginnings of a plantagenet hunch
if I stoop low beside her in the licorice dark
lay my ghost net aside and mute up
excusing her quip about my Janus head
we will hunt whatever myth she likes
swinging away from my great commission
sign me up to her new screaming front
I take full responsibility for my shining i
all the mercury the skin absorbs

EX

the keeper is living a fantasy
dream sequences are for losers these days
my job is to keep the talent tight
in the circumspect light of the compound
we attack side by side with holy aggression
we scrub the tanks before the elephants chime
nobody suspects a love story with teeth
and a smile could cause another stampede
on and on with his wobble board heart
the smell of primrose and rising damp
he always had a way of overcooking the imagery
swings and roundabouts baby—and roundabouts
he keeps waking me up to watch the lava flow
I don't care about his Italian Karate
all he ever does is spin around in circles
it's embarrassing and dangerously funny
what makes him think I won't inform
this is not a pantomime he can trust
but if he has tickets—*yes I will go*
stop wobbling it like that it will break

EXCLUDING GUNS AND AMMO

lighting beacons upon the tops of silos
sparrows fall like clods of dirt
we update our blogs according to the contract
and celebrate Christmas for cameras
excluding guns and ammo you look beautiful tonight
dumping bloated livestock into trenches
the sun still wriggling in a radio sky
always the threat of more children
but we never ask how it came to this
how some of us are immune to hanging
we never admit to stabbing dolphins for music
or to dining on the milk of weeds
excluding guns and ammo you look beautiful tonight
you don't shake when the media comes
can't we talk about us as we flog the horses
take a stab at life on the beach
tree trunks humming like old transformers
imagine spitting on the city wall or my chest
remember how babies put dead moths to mouths
the leg irons clean better with ash
excluding guns and ammo you look beautiful tonight
out there the shining bald opinions of men
lighting the beacons ingesting grams of hunger
the clods of dirt the tiny hearts

AWOL

an aurora plagues the diesel shore
more noise from the deserters' tunnel
the goat has returned to lick the salt pan
their manifesto remains botched on the wall
a tarmac tyre stack and burning crane
a troupe of players reenacting the scene
everything droning with loud speaker spirit
and suspicion like a burst water main
each of us repressing our AWOL dreams
with silky wrists for sleight of hand
what we stuff beneath the hangar curtain
before admitting we're magicians
how far can they get on a duntroon morning
why the tunnel and where will it end
why not disguise themselves as office furniture
something with theatrical merit
the role of the goat is the sticking point
might be the key to the investigation
it bleats as if accusing the chain it came from
it bleats as it wanders back in

CONFESSION

and this is where he spat in the sea
this is how he clapped for snakes
what I meant when I said *north for starters*
he tried hiding beneath kelp with bait
naming the winds he spoke of sealers
who fuck their eel-skin bags
never of cannibals who starve until
they see the house they are most afraid of
he swore he could steal me a firestick
but his balls shrank to a purse inside him
he pissed on his feet to warm them up
then his chalky feet grew cold
frogs that roared as loud as cattle
I showed him how to suck his tongue
all the time swearing on the book of Job
all the time with one eye open
I felt my head for monstrous signs
each glance a thieving octopus
until he seemed to me a lake for parting
I chewed his ears like dried apricots

UNQUENCHABLE VANDALS

if you have cancer you can just rock up
the Minister for Gulags is speaking
cursing the sick with his diamond claw
raking the air at his policy announcement
we have been named Unquenchable Vandals
for the disease of cannibalism
we prefer to call it Tickle Belly Quilting
when it tastes like chicken it's chicken
if you have cancer you can just rock up
he doesn't believe in audience burn out
he's sporting a label worn by movie stars
and the dead just have to lump it
he says we like to gingerfy everyone
and that feeding us bread will kill us
our curdled cries like a waterfall of cats
mixed with the low brass notes of the river
if you have cancer you can just rock up
we are a delectable loot of organs
trapped in the best care captivity can provide
practising our death mask expressions
none of us waiting on a passive death wish
his next target is arthritic strippers
keep watching the claw it is a magic claw
give in to its shiny diamonds

A BEAUTIFUL VILLAGE

the freshest cream is in the mouth
river rats boating the blonde
clinging to her unrealistic breasts
it used to be a beautiful village
where people read poems to bonsai trees
and mourners formed orderly queues
nobody dared throw wood in the soup
no one pissed on the sauna's hot rocks
but they tore up the stage to build a gallows
broke our legs if we kicked from the hips
guttermesh was stuffed down every throat
it used to be a beautiful village
grandmasters played chess at any hour
each year there was a pie eating contest
until the dogs began castrating themselves
every carrot grew two legs and a penis
mice were tied onto babies' clothes
horses painted with dirty lyrics
and people hated people for being fat
it used to be a beautiful village
forever the body jammed in the tree
forever the shadow in the alley
something in the bag is still alive
a jaffle iron swung in finale

DREAMLINER

the dreamliner in the bay is a gas chamber
the rowboat is returning to shore
slapping at the water's gold plate face
paddles rolling in the rowlock horns
the wherryman wears a badge-like rash
says there's a banquet on every deck
some of us are invited to dine with the captain
they are tossing our bodies starboard
think days on the river and willow trees
think parasols and panama hats
although the dreamliner is a steaming cake
the water is a channel of martyrs
the wherryman wears a badge-like rash
squeals as short as his apple knife
a child is strapped to the sing-for-me seat
an old lady is clutching at cross-stitch
we are the souls of reverse rapture
we are the last to drift upside down
a final witness of supple things
the celery top pine waving on
the wherryman wears a badge-like rash
every cruise is a new destination
triangle pillows in generous berths
and the rest is delirium

RAVINE

1.

cliffs ahead the singing ravine
a horse gallops beside the train never tiring
who is stoking the engine is the lion tame
the thorn in the paw was a dream
everything ran on grease and sequins
everybody wore a smoking hand
when Habakkuk rode into the desert
with the lighter and a wafered tongue
a trail of bunting flicks and frets
like a projectionist with a stammer
there was never a bridge the horse the horse
every boom gate is a gallows
the spitfire diving for the dining car
will the yogi come out of his trance
the jewel on his turban charging the ape
with coveting another man's wife
the ostrich's light globe head has blown
red beads across the carriage floor
a flapper girl tied to the tracks ahead
every hoof print the shape of 'you'
as the standoff continues upon the roof
three winds come clapping for hats
'and it burns burns burns the ring of fire'
there was never a bridge to be out

2.

Habakkuk rides the wincing mule
as if it matters how you travel to your funeral
everything is melting down to murder
the mirage is a cake of trouble
the Russian who said 'only blood will tell'
the sun's throwing knives never miss
may the dust you return to catch the light
who has eaten his death cap mushrooms
the mule knows the dangling carrot is a boot
the mule knows how things go around
how summer reacquaints us with our ugly feet
how Bertha pole dances in a caravan
animals in costume dream of new costumes
Habakkuk rides like prophecy
his sentence is dangling around his neck
rabbits knocking on wood in the cemetery
a tongue that tastes like the Body of Christ
and the mirage is still a cake
sometimes he hears the squeak of trees
but that must have been days ago
as somebody somewhere plays guitar
and chuckles like firewood
the bearded lady or the ringleader's wife
he should have taken the other hand

3.

it's not the storm it's the debris that kills you
in a hot chilli hallucination
eye floaters steering the eye of the film
avoid contact with the air as much as possible
people's views aside for a moment
they're calling it terminal
white goats swimming in a pool of milk
dogs nailed to the ground by thunder
the standoff continues upon the roof
smoke in the projector's beam
how to turn away from a beautiful woman
duelling with snarls and squints
the hobbled heart and violent mind
the eagle in the baby pram
the gun he draws becomes a banana
only the lighthouse keeper knows
the extraordinary life she lives without him
if they'd invested in spray on skin
the ape and mushrooms come to pass
abuse of prophecy and group hypnosis
now the only choice is how to fall
down on Habakkuk in the canyon
like a ceiling rose with a beautiful voice
about the horse about ramraid mayhem

BEAR FOREST

1.

a Harpee shot from the highest ridge
rubies and pearls from the wound
a monkey rushing the tit with a suckling gaze
a mirror propped against a tower of coins
the cloud crocodile is eaten by cloud
and the clouds smash plates together
the bear playing sax beneath the bridge
pressing keys with wedding cake fingers
grotesques roaming with cream pie cannons
the asp around the camel's neck
the milky way is a dope smoking ballerina
going from plie to plie to pirouette
a candle with a moth as a fake moustache
the Cyclops dressed in drag above the forge
a flag upon a flag and a battering ram
every night's a sleepover in the forest
it all comes down to a kerfuffle of seasons
the steaming kettle inside the bull
a black lion hunting with a mane of green fire
koi circling each other in the pond
an hourglass tumbling from a pedestal
a monkey watching itself make a crown
a carpet snake with tassels for fangs
the baby with urns for arms

2.

lust in the garden and animal dance
a tiger stroking his cock with a feather
the barking flute and brumby kings
someone's farts smell like cauliflower
entree of shutter crab and imposex snails
the weasel eating glitter in the hollow
the smirking bear in kilt and sporran
Duke of Nuts is conferred upon the squirrel
the fireside light of demonic theatre
the review of the Aberdeen Bestiary
a woodcut of Vlad the Impaler on show
above a treasure chest of lingerie
it's obvious who ate the garden rake
another cryptid with a brief cameo
devising new ways to shock the Jackalope
grenade practise with perfume bottles
no one can charm the mouse with the sword
every rib can be made into something
the bear in the kilt only answers to Mac
the squirrel declares war on almonds
herbs and trotters and the vixen comes
the forceful conversion of the lamb
the bear calls *change* and takes a bite
the hook inside the core of the apple

3.

inside is the bear and butterfly
and an owl with the face of a bear
everything is sprouting multiple heads
in search of the aphrodisiac feather
a tree mistaken for an armoured man
the bear driving the chariot
an aubergine makes an impractical hat
the deer with an eagle for antlers
cattle in robes and red blindfolds
whips goading a motor of pigs
a stallion is dancing between the flags
the bear with the flaming pubis
the cult of the bear that the bear can't join
the gaze of a lazy eyed peacock
a hand reaching out of a mountaintop
and a faun waterboarding a serpent
the lightning bolt on the broken urn
the bear reading juvenile literature
a greyhound strung above the throne
the eclipse at the tar pit fire
a prosthesis is floating upon the lake
a daisy chain necklace of nipples
the monogamous bear with a dildo nose
the broken limb behind the shield

—

the brimming
and the magic slows
the imagery of the lamb
the remnant voice upon the plains
the untangling of the word
sight and savour become no more
sight is restored to the parchment
savour reseals it with bias weight
thrashed is the hideous vision
gone is the spine with ringing barbs
thrashed is the desolation
gone is the mirror that burst into flame
the empty heart of imagination
and the egg rolls into the mountaintop
and the mountain rolls into the sea
and the sea rolls into the waiting wind
and the wind blows itself away

Printed in Australia
Ingram Content Group Australia Pty Ltd
AUHW020122021224
403587AU00003B/38

9 781925 333565